Weathering Under the Cat

poems by

Lylanne Musselman

Finishing Line Press
Georgetown, Kentucky

Weathering Under the Cat

Copyright © 2017 by Lylanne Musselman
ISBN 978-1-63534-216-1 First Edition
All rights reserved under International and Pan-American Copyright Conventions.
No part of this book may be reproduced in any manner whatsoever without written permission from the publisher, except in the case of brief quotations embodied in critical articles and reviews.

ACKNOWLEDGMENTS

These poems have appeared or are forthcoming, some in earlier versions, in the following publications:

"Bye-bye Blackbird"—*Flying Island*
"Enough is Enough"—Sleeping Cat Press Anthology
"In My First Fifty Years"—*Company of Women: New and Selected Poems*
"In My New Apartment"—*Tipton Poetry Journal*
"In the Heart of Insomnia"—*A Charm Bracelet For Cruising*
"Lost: Art"—*The Bird's Eye reView*
"Of Cats and Critics"—*Tipton Poetry Journal*
"Smothering Mother"—*The Prose-Poem Project*
"Something to Crow About"—*Company of Women: New and Selected Poems*
"Take Back Time"—*The Bird's Eye reView*
"Teddy," & "Sickly Fellow"—*Our Last Walk: Using Poetry for Grieving and Remembering Our Pets*
"Unexpected Visitor" and "Consolations After the Death of My Kitten"—*Company of Women*, and *Our Last Walk: Using Poetry for Grieving and Remembering Our Pets*.

Publisher: Leah Maines
Editor: Christen Kincaid
Cover Art: Lylanne Musselman "Weathering Under the Cat" – Mixed Media
Author Photo: Beth Mink
Cover Design: Elizabeth Maines McCleavy

Printed in the USA on acid-free paper.
Order online: www.finishinglinepress.com
also available on amazon.com

Author inquiries and mail orders:
Finishing Line Press
P. O. Box 1626
Georgetown, Kentucky 40324
U. S. A.

Table of Contents

Unexpected Visitor 1

Something to Crow About 2

Lost Art 3

The Hired Pet Sitter 4

For the Love of Cats 5

In the Heart of Insomnia 6

In My New Apartment 7

Bo 8

In My First Fifty Years 9

Smothering Mother 11

Take Back Time 12

Of Critics and Cats 14

Cats in Control 15

Enough is Enough 16

Roaring in from the West 17

Teddy 18

A Cat Perfect World 19

Bye-bye Blackbird 20

9 Lives in 13 Lines 21

Rane's Familiar 22

Sickly Fellow 23

Consolations After the Death of My Kitten 24

Pulse of a Purr 25

Dedicated to
Keli and Alison, my beloved daughters
who have shared my life along with a lot of cats
while growing up,
Styx, Tink, and Fiyero, my cats that share my life now,
and in memory of cats from my childhood throughout adulthood:
Kitti Tom, Willard, Shell, Scribbles, Bo, Jonathon, Vonne,
Vic, Katie, Ms. P., Baboo, Spice, Teddy, and Graham who passed
away while this book was in process of being published.

Unexpected Visitor

Lovers came and went,
but for eighteen years you graced my lap,
you slept next to me, and followed me
around the house. You didn't care
if the dishes were done, or if
I gained a few pounds, or shed a few tears.
You were there, a purring anchor—
even as your spirit was leaving me.

Jonathon, you came to me
in a dream last night, strong,
healthy and handsome. You
ascended the wooden stairs
coming up out of the basement,
ran into my open arms.
You reveled in my touch, I cried your name—
my one constant.

Something to Crow About

I.
The old woman wants a pet that swoops
and caws its wisdom from high
city rooftops or hidden within
the forbidden maze of cornfields.
She watches a winged flock
mock the tattered scarecrow, limp and static.
Amused, she blows kisses
in the wind, hoping one will land
on her special crow—
she holds out her hand.

II.
A young girl cuddles her tabby cat
she calls El Gato. She learned Spanish
in third grade and proudly recites
her feline knowledge to anyone who'll listen.
Cats are drawn to her and she draws cats:
fat cats, small cats, pink cats, polka dot cats,
cats with purple flowers, cats with birds in their mouths,
cats she can't know
resemble Picasso's.

III.
Two cats watch out the picture window,
twitching tails in unison, charming birds
they want as their own. The large glass reflects
their inside anxious eyes, and
the outside truths of July—
the sky blinds them blue, the mockingbird
swipes another song and the turtle doves hip hop
across their lawn.

Lost: Art

Recently at a gallery in Chicago,
David asked: "When did you become interested in art?"

He didn't know, in 1962, my kindergarten teacher
pulled mother aside because of a ladybug I'd drawn,

or that I'd won first place in third grade
for my abstract picture of a cat, á la Picasso,

or that my high school art teacher revered my work,
assured my doubting mother I had talent.

David didn't know my love of art gave me a high
that drugs never did, and saved me, more than once,

from adolescent suicide, or that art held my hand
through three divorces and dark, pitched nights.

He didn't know I'd become torn between the pull
of painting portraits and the constant tug of words, or

that my perfectionism refused art's invitations to play.
How could he know I pushed my first love away?

The Hired Pet Sitter

I expected timid Scribbles
to hide, and for Vonne and Jonathon
to show their faces and
greet the pet sitter for food and treats.

Upon returning home, what I didn't expect
was to receive report cards
for my three furry children.
Vonne got an A.

My bright Jonathon, a B,
although social, he was too vocal, but
it was Scribbles who received
the worst grade a big red F.

I will never forget the feeling
of humiliation when finding my cat
is a failure in the pet sitter's eyes
just because she was unsociable
and didn't play well with others.

For the Love of Cats

As a child I begged my dad, "let me have a cat"
and for years he never answered.
In the meantime, for my kitty fix, I visited cats
from my neighborhood, and checked out cat library books.

As an adult I faced lovers who hated cats—
an ex-husband who hated cats so much that whenever he saw one
near the road he gunned the car to hear me scream. After the divorce
I let my young daughters choose their first cat, Scribbles, and
we collected cats until we had Bo, Jonathon, Katie, Vic, and Ms. P.

My girls grew up and moved, and our cats lived out their lives
with me. But still, with cats in tow, I moved in with one lover
who threw Bo up against the wall for keeping her awake.
Another could not accept my cats sleeping in our bed,
she believed purring was growling, and hated cat fur.

Now, I live in a small apartment with my two black cats, siblings
Graham and Tink, and young Fiyero. We live in constant companionship—
with no one to threaten or shout when one lies on top of the refrigerator,
licks tuna salad from my plate, or drinks water in the kitchen sink.

In the Heart of Insomnia

> *In the Heart of the Heart of the Country*
> *William H. Gass*

It's the heart of winter, two a.m.
in the heart of Indiana,

in the heart of the bed,
Maggie snuggles next to me

deeply breathing her dreams,
and I'm on the edge

listening to freezing rain chatter
February on our window pane,

low flying jets,
gliding west at three-thirty a.m.,

trains whistle me awake,
weary words crisscross my mind,

form erratic lines in search of a poem,
I weave in and out of insomnia,

weathering under the cat
purring sleep across my belly.

In My New Apartment

for Maggie

If I would've died last night,
when the crack whore was down
the hall beating on a neighbor's door,
screaming "You punk ass bitch!
Open up! Let me in, Bob!" over and over,
and I didn't know if bullets would fly, and
I didn't know if she'd knock and pound her way here,
and I didn't know my cats could
pussyfoot so lightly in the middle of the night,
without a creaky croak from the hardwood floor,
I would've died happy, after
spending the evening with you, finding us
again, my head peacefully upon your breast,
listening to your heart thump, thump, thumping loud.

Bo

Bo's furred chin rested on my forehead
as the alarm clock pushed me into the day.
On my way to Chicago, I dropped him
at the vet for a routine teeth cleaning.
That morning Bo had casually walked into his carrier.
I didn't have to fight him like I did with Scribbles who threw a mean bitch slap,
or Jonathon who spread his back legs like the span of eagle wings
and did a little voodoo dance.

All day I thought of Bo, and knew that his teeth would be the envy
of my other cats. I left Chicago singing "It's a great day to be alive"
along with Travis Tritt on the radio. As I drove closer to my exit
my cell phone rang. It was the vet, and nothing prepared me for:
"He didn't make it, I'm sorry. He had a hidden health problem.
What do you want done with his body?"
That night the other cats looked for Bo.

In My First Fifty Years

I have seen the sky knitting
its cover with strings of light.
I have seen squirrels tumble,
clowns of the lawn.
I have seen the seven of clubs,
flipped face up, trump my thoughts.
I have seen my black kitten's head stuck
in a milk crate so tight
he looked as if he was being convicted
at a witch trial.
I have seen my own heart break
in time to build room
for real love.
I saw reality TV
40 years before its popularity—
Lee Harvey Oswald's
final face, grimaced,
shot dead, live on camera.
I have seen poverty
pick its own sweet pockets.
I have seen police
high speed through low limits
in their leisure suits.
I have seen my love drunk
in a twelve-step dance
with addiction.
I have seen Chatty Cathy
lose her voice
in a game of Tiddlywinks
against Uncle Wiggly.
I have seen September
shed leaves, and chill my lattes cold.
I have seen my stretched skin
marked by the drum
of the womb.
I have seen people shuttered
by an image.

I have seen a dying page
breathe on its own.

Smothering Mother,

remember when you forced me to sit on that red stool for hours. You pushed and pulled my hair into ringlets. I squirmed in your firm "hold still!" You made me wear dresses and patent leather shoes, and never let me swing upside down on monkey bars. I stayed in my room, listened to stacks of 45s, read Nancy Drew, and confided in stuffed Huckleberry Hound and Bugs Bunny. My school friends were not allowed in our house: Jackie too plump and Janet too wild for Church Street where Shirley Temple ruled. But that day when Mrs. Gannon, fat with religion, came to our door, I listened to her scold you for not allowing me to jump rope in her yard you thought was filled with mangy cats and dead grass. At home you called her mussed-up daughters "Edie, Audey, and Ugly." I hated when they called me "Curly" in public. Outside, her children played filthy with laughter, while I sat "ladylike" somber, inside.

Take Back Time

Give me back my grandma's voice
weaving words, threading my mind,
unfolding tapestry of our heritage.
Give me back the days
spinning a stack of 45s
in Davy's room,
discovering "Pretty Woman,"
singing along with Roy Orbison,
no regrets.
Give me back my hard thighs
flying over the hurdles of my youth.
Give me back my ability to eat a Whopper at noon,
drink regular Coke all day,
indulge in pie on a whim,
never gaining an ounce.
Give me back my passion for painting
before repetition turned to cinders,
canvassing the country
selling art for profit.
Give me back the happiness in the whiskers
of my cat's chin, lying on my forehead
prior to his passing
to perch on a cosmic cloud.
Give me back years wasted
married to men I did not love
for reasons not yet acknowledged.
Take back the years of being stupid,
never being able to do anything right
because my daughters' father said so.
Take back the years of trying to please
anyone who was not me.
Take back the years of lying
under the weight
of my conscience banging the headboard.
Take back the dresses I despised,
frilly and femme, unflattering,
never finding a hem I could tolerate.

Give me back the friendly manner
I possessed until I locked the door
after too many knocks
from those that entered
before I was ready.
Give me back.

Of Critics and Cats

Life is difficult with a live-in critic who stifles creativity
every time my hand finally moves across the page,
after sitting for hours anticipating inspiration,
and whispers, "that sucks."
I try to ignore her, but she's even more persistent
than a cat after tuna!
I can't escape her,
after all, she's looking out for my best interests—
I don't want to embarrass myself
by writing something silly
like the *wings of ducks stir the river*
like a spoon in won ton soup.
Wincing, I think of all of the poets I admire
and, with my live-in critic's help,
I'm sure they never had any trouble
writing a great poem the first time their pen
touched paper or their typewriter tapped out
words that unlocked their futures.
Then I sit, wheels stuck spinning
and flipping mud like shit on my thoughts,
turning them into metaphors that stink
as much as my critic says I do.
So I succumb to my critic's suggestion
that no one cares what I write,
put my pen down, let good ideas fade away,
and go feed my cat more tuna.

Cats in Control

I can't wait to get back home and relax
after a long day of meetings and teaching,
my three beloved cats are waiting there patiently
for affection and feeding, attention and treats.

After a long day of meetings and teaching
I look forward to eating, relaxing, and watching TV,
for affection and feeding, attention and treats—
my cats demand I toss toys or laser light tease them all.

I want nothing more than to eat, relax, and watch TV,
instead my cats have their own plans for me
they demand I toss toys or laser light tease them all
shining that red dot across the hardwood floors and up the wall.

My cats always have their own plans for me—
as soon as I sit down with my plate to eat and relax, they want
that red dot to shine across the hardwood floor and up the wall
before I can even eat my own meal, or turn on the TV.

As soon as I sit down with my plate to eat and relax, they want—
my three beloved cats are waiting for me impatiently,
before I can even eat my own meal, or turn on the TV.
Still, I can't wait to get back home and eventually relax.

Enough is Enough

Storms have always been a nemesis
across Mother Earth, but here in the Midwest
they pick on us—
imposing bullies who won't quit
until we cry "uncle,"
forcing us to dig deeper storm cellars,
build higher levees,
and restock disaster supply kits.
We plan our escapes,
flash storm watches and warnings,
see the hopeful rainbow—
so we stick it out, vulnerable,
surrounded by corn and bean fields,
helpless as the cows and horses,
but it's only a matter of time
before thunderheads boil across the horizon,
smother the sun and propel winds into killers—
uproot century-old trees, trample flowers,
flood crops, slay livestock, and ransack our homes.
We return from our hideouts to find
that signed copy of *Breakfast of Champions* destroyed,
that photo of Aunt Mildred ruined,
the neighbor's Chevy Silverado flipped into town hall,
that manuscript, nearly complete after twenty-five years, gone,
and, Tabby, missing for days,
crawls out from under the overturned armoire.

Roaring in from the West

Thunderstorms grumble
and hiss in June.
Squirrels pirouette
and song sparrows scatter.

Ready to rumble,
restless Mother Nature
tosses her substantial
weight around.

In screened windows,
unfazed, my cats
weather weary,
watch the rain
whip and splatter.

Teddy,

my little Jonathon clone, how can you be so alike without ever walking the earth at the same time? Jonathon left me at eighteen years old, two days before Christmas in 2007; you came to me at four months old, a week after my birthday in 2011. Did his spirit find a way back to me? I'm not sure I believe in such things, but when I saw that humane society photo of you in the *Toledo Free Press*, I lost my heart to your heart shaped face, your tabby cat coat, those almond eyes; the line about you getting your name from cuddling with your teddy bear. I thought you'd be scooped up in someone else's arms before I had the chance to come for you. A week and a half passed before I could get life to slow down enough and to prep my other two kitties, for your possible arrival. When I called the shelter you were still there. Was it a miracle or a karmic sign? When we first met, you put your little head in the palm of my hand and purred loudly. Back home, you made yourself familiar in my lap. That night you rubbed your tiny head against my cheek over and over again, brushing away my tears.

A Cat Perfect World

A life without cats
is unthinkable,
unfathomable, imperfect.
In a cat perfect world
felines rightfully would be
worshipped as poet
Rane Arroyo called them:
Buddhas with fur.

Cats would not be
marginalized by naysayers
as evil occult pushers
by those humans
who peddle their cat hatred
to any soul they can stroke.

Cat lovers don't buy
that heartless view—
the cost too high
to lose companions
of the most distinguished
kind—those knowing eyes,
warming purrs, the honor
of a trophy gift at your feet.

Bye-bye Blackbird

> To *Wounded Bird and Cat, 1938*—Picasso

The cat's
bloated belly
fades into
the blues—
a blackbird,
once vibrant
and free,
now limp,
feathers plucked—
unsung music
from a beak
agape, its
last song
fed black
cat's hunger
for winged beauty,
plump breast,
wishbone.

9 Lives in 13 Lines

Your eyes intrigue me, my pet
black cat. I refuse the feline evil
beliefs where you do biddings for witches,
cast spells with your stares

of golden green eyes. Black magic
dating back to when Salem was un-bewitching,
thinking—Puritan politics
that we're still not thankful for.

For some, nine lives bring joy
with pets and purrs. For some nine lives
are lived bullied and hated. For simply being
an other—accused, abused, and killed.
Black, white, striped—still.

Rane's Familiar

Selena, I look at you
and see Rane. Not
because Glenn told me
Rane said you were "his
familiar," not because
you are stubborn and
have the talent to get every human
to do what you want, not
because you can scare
three out of four kittens into doing good,
not because your eyes show wisdom
(of at least eight of your nine lives left),
not because you are smooth and easy on the eyes—
but because I see your love for Glenn,
how you make him alive
with Rane now gone and how
you make their house his home.

Sickly Fellow

When I picked him up
from the Humane Society,
I worried what I'd done—
my older cats so predictable
and now there'd be new kitten antics—
him swinging from curtains, clawing his way
up furniture or knocking over the flat screen TV.

Instead I got this sickly fellow,
who sleeps away the days,
who loves to snuggle, but has health issues
expected with older cats, not a seven-month-old.

Now diagnosed with pneumonia,
he's had more meds in three months
than my previous ten cats combined.
How I wish for the worry of shooing my kitten
off of curtains or mending snagged furniture.

Consolations After the Death of My Kitten

> *"After James Tate's 'Consolations After an Affair'"*

Chattering at shadows on the ceiling,
my cats run room to room.
They see little Teddy.
As we settle down at night, he visits.
And I can hear peaceful cats purring,
the love that moves me.
I've discovered that I don't need
a lousy spouse, a loan to repay.
I have unfinished paintings
that wait for van Gogh to return.
They know nothing of sangria and Vonnegut.
For them a foggy night in February
is a ghost of an excuse.

Pulse of a Purr

This morning I woke
with comfort and
an emotional jolt.
The unexpected
chin of my three
year old cat, Fiyero,
resting peacefully on
my forehead. A feeling
I have not had for fourteen
years; since my cat, Bo,
who regularly slept with me
this way, passed on
to his cosmic cloud,
even three cats that
shared my life with Bo
never picked up their chins
for this snuggly habit, but
it's this ornery newcomer,
who since a baby chose
to sleep on the edge
of the bed, or near my feet,
until this sacred Sunday he
surprised me with a familiar
baptismal pulse of a purr.

Lylanne Musselman is an award-winning poet, playwright, and artist. A native Hoosier, she recently moved back to Indianapolis, after living in Toledo, OH, and Ypsilanti, MI. Her work has appeared in *cahoodahoodaling, Pank, Flying Island, The Rusty Nail, New Verse News,* and *So it Goes, Issue 3,* among others, and many anthologies, including the forthcoming *Our Last Walk: Using Poetry for Grieving and Remembering Our Pets* (University Professors Press, 2016). A twice nominated Pushcart Prize nominee, Musselman is the author of three previous chapbooks, and she co-authored *Company of Women: New and Selected Poems* (Chatter House Press, 2013). Presently, she teaches writing of all stripes at IUPUI, and Ivy Tech Community College.

www.ingramcontent.com/pod-product-compliance
Lightning Source LLC
LaVergne TN
LVHW041518070426
835507LV00012B/1659